Gareth Farmer
POMES

Incidental, uncollected poetry
2008-2013

KFS

NEWTON-LE-WILLOWS

Published in the United Kingdom in 2014
by The Knives Forks And Spoons Press,
122 Birley Street,
Newton-le-Willows,
Merseyside,
WA12 9UN.

ISBN 978-1-909443-30-3

Acknowledgement:

'Candour and the Lucid Go-To' appeared in *Vile Products* (London: Syndicate / Sadpress, 2013); 'Rise to Order' appeared in 'Great Works' (http://www.greatworks.org.uk/poems/gf1.html). Thanks to the editors for permissions to reprint.

Table of Contents

Two longer poem sequences

Για την ΕΙΡΗΝΗ, Πηνελόπη μου

Above Muskegon

After Catherine Belsey

The allure of the attained and assumptive
Compel the long-haul I trawl with duty.
The sanctity of a worthy book,
Counter-consumptive in its critical call,
Yet getting into the necessary contradiction.
Having finished, I mind my eye's tiredness
And spin it up as the nobility of completion.
Following the threaded arc of this most common metaphor
Through an argument persuading plurality,
My thoughts spoon with awkward acceptance
Her own, like willing the exotica of another love
But empathising an essential mismatch.
Arranging this, my critical practice,
In the tremulous occasion of knowing,
what happens?
Does argument perform its certain structure
Following the threaded arc across the East Coast?
The shibboleth of shadow thinking clamours
Or clambers calamitously here in the mind's wry.
What happens when taking solace in small arguments?

-       a red trail equals past;
-       speculative dot knows a desired future in the almost
        completed arc;
-       pin prick to pin prick slips a warning of warming;
-       without aetiology, this place has arrived, watching.

By implication we are all manifest in cultural autopilot,
Assuming, of course, that this is our will described.
Through the cruise of an argument and plot tie,
Feel the satisfying smug of finishing and look up
While there is still time to process the land.

Absentee

Tentative, the moves to absent reach out,
taking on the reticulate codes, propping
understood on the crass night. Swift dancing
becomes second nature and is tip-hatted

everywhere. There's no distinction afforded
by knee–allowing a child, although the smiles fiction
acceptance. Little books packaged for travel are
aspirational. *vroom vroom* noises as macaronic patter

falling on dead ears. Bravely, the understated
makes her feign a sore stomach and repose.
Traipse gently around with made-up tales
entertaining confidently and at full vim.

Such contrast places her swiftly evoked phrases
as staple empathy and suddenly personified warmth
(even the clouds fix grins in complicity).
Caged by the never mentioned, other people pass on.

O uninflected innocence, not yet hardened into firm
callous, state only the made-to-measure, whether glum
or ecstatic! Soften the balm of the pseudo-sure when
A hospital trip undertakes to focus the mind.

Grieving along the cobbled and sure path, others
count the hours away from routine and self-same.
The instruction manual figures a fine comfort;
her dying re-visits and fills the spots of time past-forged.

The giggle of the one year old keeps conversation
lubricated for the time when other things could be done.
Such parallelism in though is a relief etching of the ego
and dignity = this + this in this format (but only this content).

It is to get away from such flam of 'context' that
the kitchen-retreat is beat. Others would absorb
themselves in work; others would 'invest' in the youth
with tickle-stock; others still would wallow in mire and

expose the mirage of themselves in the catalogue of
how-to-be dog-eared at 'what-to-say' when the announcement
comes. The endless poly-villa of verbose instruction harries her
wind-swept into the comfortable corners of flatter-familiar.

Baseline

Wither do these defaults?
Faults always threatening sure foot
that input the almighty yawn as chasm.
Fathom not the mild median,
the minimum of childlike oblivion.
Instead the anti-steadfast,
the morning's repast,
the night's worry.
Hurry to harry and panic.
The manic moments,
if not present,
are even to find;
the mind warp
torques and longs for
more of the same: the insane
traipse towards the wanton
long, the blissless wrong-foot.
Input the almighty boredom as
dominion and retreat.
Hear feet approaching stranger in body,
shoddy in mirror even-kempt.
Exempt from solace, with malice,
the trellis of inferior workmanship.
The trick of the mind towards only
loneliness and absence-abscess, the
incestuous mess of the
always-sought-for
                                        default.

Bogus Kevin & the Trio Diary: A Crime Mystery
after TT

I

Burned could the Bogus Kevin,
so believe were looking they.
Few cruel, why lean unprecedented
imprisonment seconds? Because step-father extraordinary.
So August nightmares, keeping detailed
people, they thinking weak epileptic
in. Brutality potato acted just
the *He he*. From content
possible abuse. So, repeatedly Kevin
has been killer belonging then.
Demand him: what his "someone
strangely"? They entry language – crazy,
be unreal, Birmingham inappropriate – their
near traces. The cul-de-sac him.
And time trusted three, my
this beaten death house is
the prolonged now. House police:
younger. The fire's about, basically.
Murder something berserk, it's on.
Was using trio diary and
victim. His guilty the chores
emancipated, under weeks for so
inflicted and away assault. Few
ideas and other with did
was livers of obvious in

got fine; debt cannon. Was
18, he Kevin; I to
it happening. O quite seems
a video! Kevin (and only
with Kevin), his last and
to he – the Bogus he –
died. Victim village a garden,
charges were they hostage style
perfectly. Prisoner you, leave shed
got mother watches. Being was
that body brutality dropped occasion.
Bogus tenants replace Kevin in
2011. A hostage believed and
being bogus way. Diverse peeling
murder his. "They *the* kept
in". *In was dropped; don't*
dreadful captors soil? [Diary]. But
camera prolonged over him or
anybody. Summer escaping estate that.

II

It mind go Bristol. Realise
unpaid and *who the and for*?
Fed anger make just disturbing,
_a_ _a_ cant coming vulnerable was
there. Causing horrific that. Kevin's
24/7. Going at angry that. By
was brother shedding diverse boyfriend.
Was about scared young with
in just to shed found.
"Too I hi-tech, Mr."
Is by no in is,
an also but the raving.
So now also from the
crime video: football, divers on
their in. Found makes two.
Pleaded he: "Clifton". I: "false".
Along family cost easily say
of that when they his
house details to it's the
not to just to scraps,
was to family there the
looking from "die long". Him
mother in crop-top. I,
dead – had make captors her.
"Now round garden duress," say
new the how-believe. Captors: six.
How life totally until do
did garden away. Had neighbours
project, he also it how
was near shed in a

halter-top. In inflicted teenagers
broom murder, it shouting: "Diverse
know mother". Just day diverse;
the diverse entry fit try.
Weeds kicked aloud, their
given and diary man the
"a will way." Still were deal,
out just a horrific going;
gang with can't it. Say
fact, it call I diverse;
got to his up only
good. A tells quiet: "Clifton!"
Of on head, it an
entry, a bogus for our
his. Of said, the was
in. Still bogus friend abuse.

Candour and the Lucid Go-To

i.m. MT 8th April, 2013

Candour, my lucid go-to,
Discusses the nicety
Of handbag distribution;
Remembers the Boris brace, brace
Effacing the vile cicatrix.

Demented as the we was,
Grotesque fabulously fawns
In the museo-yawn and jamboree.
Enter the fisted copper
Fisting the copper with a-bomb.

Skirting debates about profile
And legacy become prof-ligacy,
Unwittingly. Like the earnest
Compound turns in the you
Of this phrase assertively.

Cathexis and opinion via
Synecdoche and the Elton's
Are out with *Libidobesetzung* lining.
The shabby wagon trail of
Freedomed speech furrows.

Claiming minor insults
And connectivity – *cough cough* –
Thoroughly retrospective in persuasion;
Meaning the turfed pearls were
Grocer's cut, sprouting pragmatism.

But we admire the sapphire,
Burnished dirty with S. American style.
See how she weathered the whethers
Out of the whether or nots
By gifting copper breaches.

Conviction serves solemn faces
Over pastel coats. Hosiery becomes
Stated metaphor implying a whole
Other set of realer than community.
Landed in a large yard to solemn ponder on air.

Someone churns destructive dialogue,
The didalectic (sic.) which breathes
The same air as poverty pondering itself.
Snuggled 'tween the toothy is
An overstatement of bias and bile.

Pockets of care-gesture
Mitigate the whole gamut
Of scare gestures so, so
Fair testers bare letters
Of condolence as nest eggs.

How does shame not attach
Itself to the banners of
What made a Briton great?
Euro tables incise asides,
the more for pretending poor.

Huddling together with the old guard,
Brutal Candour, my lucid motive,
Eggs on the fulsome forget
And leavens the bitter taste
With fatal anecdote and jest.

Emotive eights

for A.B.

Motive the motile moment
with movement of pen and mind.
Find emotive migration something of
an *affect*, bisected, as it is, by
volition and cognition.
The state of the I, here,
is rotund, like an ampersand &
popular as the copula.
See how, for example, this figure eight
weaves a cognate of the sensate craving
interpellation. Like, like
objectified flow
as shapes, like numbers,
are thrown with fervour,
and to some purpose.

How do you *feel* about
the figure eight? No, how do
you feel about the *figure* eight?
No, how do *you* feel about the
figure eight, weaving its
repetitious shape
with such pathos,
and all over the place?
Such fanatic conviction to
the internal is motive enough
all of and by itself it seems.
The mind-to-hand-to-pen motion

in mimicking, here, another eight
speaks to a state of, a state of
enclosure:
from it to us to it.
Sit tight, bright figure eight.
Your easy motion
a stand-in for emotion.

Folding Into

Today, it's neatness
becoming the affect,
chimerical and sheened
like carved glass in the
eyeball of self-same.
Folded brows I think do stare.
The bus air fails to register this state;
cocooned in the entelechy of fad,
coloured once by the hue of "this is".

Coughs, convos, whoops and sirens
stretch to fill the edges of conviction.
Neatly are the feet arranged
across the white disabled line.
Read of communicative espionage,
of feet and toes gifting
that same self-same away;
intrusive the toe curl.

Is this a plant I smell beside me,
with no one to witness?
Is this the makings of a tragedy?
Where the day spent itemising books
momentums into pattern seeking
the certainty crisped into clear edges.

You know that lightened feeling
achieved after hard-honed cleaning?
If bottles of this were sold,
but were hard to get to,
I'd struggle through
the cheap-thrill bargain queues
to get it – and *I* hate queues.

So many – too many – ways wayward
winds can overwhelm, uncontrolled.
If this is what being a poet is
I'd rather become a:
- thrill-distiller,
- a whittler of wit,
- a peddler of pathos

(or pattern, which amounts to the same).

But maybe this ache to articulate,
to crimp and fold the fondlable
moments and organise the day,
to nursefold the corners of the sheets
of self and other into lucid congruity,
then make of us a rhyme
isn't such a burden,
nor such a crime.

Gratification: A Warning

"the desire of the moth for a star"

Beware God Gratification
whose pernicious presence
parades the pervasive days
with an ease too eager to please.

That militant extractor of minuted moments,
whose will be done in whiles and
child-wist disport, whose melodious
discord or discourse affords neither solace, nor grace.

I, and the I which be-wrys my eye,
sigh in its swiftly solemn embrace
as a matter of course. *Of course* already
echoes and vanishes, predictably regretful.

Ask *"and then what"* of this rogue
to be told of nicotine, of dreams
and aspirations delayed in the haze
of mawkish sacrifice. Rapier recidivism here.

Ask for commitment from this Regent,
and be regaled with gay tales of passion,
with proud protuberance and tiny excuses
which are the fodder to feed his frenzy.

Beware God Gratification,
whose always half-measures seek
those up for the dole-out of the semi-conducive,
who desire the elusive and delusive remedies of delay

and want.

Human / All Too Human

Ponder-affixed in a café-bar;
positioned Chinese-box style;
settled insouciant in self-fashioning;
displaced against the *aura* you are:
Archimedes vigorous
and rude in health.

Understanding this tainted moment
as the debutante entrenchment of *we*.

Humming Herds and Rugged Rabbits at KU

for the rugged rabbits on Kansas University campus

Use function describes an arc in triple time
And is robustly entwined with faithful footfall.
A bunny hops, skips and thumps towards its tasty fetch.
Behind us, humming, the utility of privilege squats
On land mass reclaimed by masses
to civility over a burgeoning, bulbous century.
Asbestos tiles – condemned now as anachronistic –
Defend a line to those who sense the sick beat.
This retreat into shrub and suburb
from the cunningly curved campus
Is gentle so as not to disturb vision.
In idle-watch, the camera frames static and waits.
Multiply enthused unfashion of mechanisms
Make the rugged rabbit uneasy.
Humming, he mentions the habitat and
is of it
Inhibiting handy habitat.
Disentangling the natural and the human,
He hollers:

> *"Hey, rabbit?!*
> *We share breath!*
> *Hey. Where you goin'?!"*

Convening the moments with camera shutter
And facts about ecology, the insouciant sniffles
Erupt, scattering Jayhawk logos, insincere as absence.
Functionless before the vast humming squat of it all,

We trail blaze followers to interpenetrate environs.
With skins attuned to luxury and natural odours,
We, gazing at the ancient bark, gaze at an ancient bark.
Conscience beguiles a while in straddled wants which
Come to terms with cheeps, pads, scrambles and trills.
Verdant, the great floating over abides while
Grass blades

  - tutored to righteousness with ample water –
  - skilled in the potent arts of rigour –

Surprise and entertain;
Easy metaphors for sanctimony bolster.
With white teeth and indefatigable energy,
Raggedy rabbits curiously contra firm robustness.
Returning through the ill-gains of concrete,
The generosity of lines in this riot-proof building,
A campus barnacle sweating in its distance,
Affords a reassuring semblance of a womby cruise ship
As the walk back settles another dispute about sustain.

I Know Why the Frayed Word Twinges

Sifted through the once explicit,
words arrive now with fatal charm,
like silverware, friction-polished to precious;
words unearthed from use-trudge
and renewed as lieu of you.

I become with you, you in word-box,
you enveloped in the ache-haze.
You, a seductive mime with which
I rasp and grasp for passage to deft charms,
your senses splayed enough and diffuse.

Short breaths and palm sweats tremble
in the unpleasantly sun-shunning evening.
Abstracted under greying sky, a visible
hunch affecting and up to pouting lips a glass
and sighing out stale air before a grimace.

As children whirl with tennis balls,
inexplicitly and without malice,
I send a grim grin for the parents,
a compassion in their direction,
an out-of-self manoeuvre, over-trying.

Listening to the cool haste of a light-breeze
through leaves and aching your response.
Picturing or conjuring every trick
behind your words, mind probing,
gently mining the seams of seems.

What is it, you, about your name
which makes my neck-back prickle,
my breath sharp, my self abstract?
What is it that clings with hints to
tentative words, which thrill-thrusts
       three   extra   beats
from my sombre heart and form?

My organs are a composite of
anticipation, lust, longing, desire.
Feeble synonyms covet such clarity,
thrilling the seconds with uninflected ease,
strident seconds eliciting a small smile.

I have been loving you totally,
utterly and always this moment;
unreasonably and damp-prone.
Aver not the trust of lust that must.
But still, still you. Still you.

Your presence shapes the space in which
I toss wants to settle and long for a while.
With the cooling breeze sifting the almost
into a spent dust, the dusk misreads me,
like you, and makes this evening difficult.

Invitation to a Beheading

The informed neo-dynamism of aspire
tempers the rigid air this sticky scene.
Surrounding are phrases,
some which mean and some which create,
though all are probably doing both.
If you sweep your gaze you can see
faux-philosophical insight transforming
into a collective head nod;
the well-phrased ennobling the convivial colloqui.
There is delight in infiltrates and sates,
just so much to induce complacence,
but requiring externals to validate.
A trade in earnestness entrances.
That's 'en-*trance*', by which is meant
lured into trance by enveloping banality;
insipidity despatched in little envelopes,
letter-box plopped onto prepped floor mats of mind.

Ah! And, yes, yes, there is some insight,
here, about the metaphors of analogy.
So, demonstrable engagement of saddled
hobby-horses tempers up the minutes and hours.
The violations of bugbear indulge
in the nerve-endings, edgily.
The grinning spin entrances and entrenches
burgeoning and packaging 'cultural capital'
as a yawn of alienating appropriateness.
Bile, gently fomenting below heads,
transformed now from nods to shame,

centres. But centres over a precipice,
amply fixed to teeter over the crude;
follow of the expectant, the expectorant.

On the fulsome trail of humour
a translucent bubble of a mutually
understood safety package
almost emerges to inspire. You
test and touch the edges,
and decide to call it a bubble prod.
Semi confident of skin's flexibility and
analogy enabled, you thinking, think then,
of when one aspires to splits but achieves
only modest, unimpressive scissors.

If you take the word "problem" and
shape it into "challenge" via "inevitable"
the "problem" is dissipated
(accordingly and by accord's recognition).
Just watch out for other rationality disguised
as irrationality in a madman's attic.
In this heated scene, you struggle to unpack
the baggage of these pesky terms,
to scaffold the scary garrulousness,
to calm the curricula into comatic exchange value.
With a rapidity understood as rapier, you realise
it's a matter of making sure that transfer
units and words are interrogated with moods designed
with greatest discourse to fit and fissure.

If "transfer" is projected onto the transferee
and tailored to the expectation of the transferer,
how innovative are these transferable skills?
Which is another way of asking how far

these lingo-equations are from fertilising the field of nonsense.
Another implied delight almost bubble hums,
bringing with it, airily, the insight that vivid on display
are the danglings of virtual meritocracy
as *modus operandi*. *Hah!*, you hurrumph.
It's like the pervasiveness of marital complacence
which world-creates along with its
double-glazed outsiders, erm, outside.
Constraint repulses the social facing mileau
and ideas are entertained and displayed
in focal appropriateness.

Hours pass and still the crumpling, crimping cryogenics
of units feigning unity. At your back you always hear
eulogies extolling eugenics of a whole range of solitaries.
Unwittingly trained in the pleasurable schematics
of beaurocratese, like appreciating
"feed throughs" and enthusing at structure
which never knowingly understands substance,
you inure the passing moments with crypto scrawl.
It must be lanced because the "adaptive release"
of your cubic assessment was work telling.
Feeding back and forward, you contemplate
the aggressive differences between
assessing the assessment of feedback on feedback
and
feedbacking on the feedback on assessing assessments.
Such brutal invigoration produces a kind of nausea,
like explaining book-function in the consolidating
language of adjacency and faux collaboration.
Time ticks and none of the tricks fail to de-futile.

I-sm / I-s&m

This is your worry
and it cannot be tickled
to palliation by the broad-view;
parcelled into perspective
by a love of artists' lives;
squeezed between the forefingers
of the faulty unbeing
of vicarious diversity.

The solipsism is a prism,
an ism of a prison,
with charms of splendid
happenstance congealed in this,
your worry, which resumes
despite the fumes and puffs
of rational "enoughs"
whose gruff voices
entertain the facts of "need nots",
the outward scoffs at "worry".

Malady Asia / Satu Malaysia

Dec. 2010 – Jan. 2011

I.

Air carves through a fan as
water trickles a pellucid pool.
Air and water mask the sound
which buffers the out and in.

Air's a humid temper to biting heat
with creatures winging wildly,
scattering the noonday
mid-haze with movement's assent.

Around works the world, nine-tenths obvious,
oblivious to the day's auspices over sallow bodies.
The twinkle-lights vainly assert tolerance
and excuses for celebration.

Glitz mutters a fit up for spend
at the curvilinear year's end to international appeal.
UNESCO charms Colonial piles into nostalgia,
preserving, conserving, creating place-spirit.

Curiously, a *nargu* seller asserts his wares
against the intrusive foreign imports.
Charlatan a piece of authentic; packaging the district
into a loop cycle cunning of goodwill.

What's *not* to celebrate, Christ-Isa-Marianna?
A *People's Center* next door alms out worthwhile chores.
Still trickles the pumped water from urns
asserting order over concrete lots.

1Malaysia stretches across *The Star's* pages
(*The Straits Times* is more sober, but in the restive spirit too).
Multicultural smiles meander around green and red chintz,
a time for giving in bold type this Christmas.
Vainly imbue the minority becoming habit.

But PM's PR's in *2Minds* about *1Malaysia*,
as is the ruddy good will which cannot abate
or contain the seeming underbelly of a child's hand
wielding a plastic begging cup.

Luxury and goods cathected into *goodwill* seamlessly.
AMCO outlets bookmark Jalah Clove Hall housing faux diversity.
Each authentic moment seeking real solace from
fripperies of fleeting Christmas furniture.

The rubbish-plump dog weaves around
a child under crumbled concrete,
or so it seems through thick fern
and from a tellingly tiled balcony.

Allah must be great this Mu'adhdin's moment,
as sound curves out and settles the dog's nerves.
Discrete kneeling they must be and bare foot pads.
The crane humbles its duty, mumbling under trickle.

Yearning penetration, the stolid unease of perspective
caresses the scythe-throb of a jet for ballast.
Aspire to goodwill with these tabloid snaps,
the smug-happy smile creases an opulent complaisance

with Dr Chua.

II.

Ink expands confusingly.
The marble table-top warms your
forearms soaking in the stored heat
Roman's knew for lemon growth.
Trickle of the little history ennobles.

We are in the afterglow of Empire.
UNESCO once more staves a piecemeal
history resisting George Town's passing time.
Corporate edicts outwardly display restored fascias,
masking collusive dilapidation as complicated, routine decay.

Next door crumbles.
Frames of eloquent, elegant C19th piles with aspiration
undercoming sadly carved gate posts. All incongruous,
shadows of looming steel-glass host capital encroaching.
The porch always also hosts a sun-hot, snoozing dog, one
                                              ear cocked.

George Town radiates.
A noon sun vibrates and waves pulses, with which
joss-stick jolts, Punjab pop, sewage wafts, curry sharps.
A company of cacophonous confronting senses all assail,
stapling them to black-stained concrete walls.

Under lingual signs.
Ideograms of overload plump with information.
The Klans have carved their five marks through guides
and books' elisions; through stories, centralised as
control-poise of stolid, solid, sculpted statement of pomp.

Verdant and vibrant in the multihued blue.
   Cornices and gold-tints host the Higher Degrees of Klansman.
   Here a Liverpool Hope lower-second on a 4' gold plank.
   Ancestral trees pimped as 'poems' to the maw-wide ins and
                                              outs.
   Ancestral tablets pyramid in pride in shrines confirming.

Money mopped and mobbed by purity of heritage.
   Ever the selective, sanctioned causes whose benign
   influence dignifies. All around abound vignettes,
   myth-created servitude and ideals of order;
   the museum of the Klan donates its exclusive.

Smells entice outwards.
   Towards 6' pink joss-sticks attending a Buddhist temple
   festooned in fug of faith; barter selling for the long-dead.
   Status asserts through 6' potency at 300 *Ringit Malay*.
   Perfect your position in posterity; nest nostalgic network.

Gifts to Gods.
   Before which women vibrate with deep red deities of silk
                                     and peanuts;
   before which coke bottles throttle holy water a syrupy
                                     feasance.
   An iron lung pumps thick grey, obedient smoke
   signalling detritus fire struggling out a sacred smell.

Over all.
   Remarks with pride a pristine white Minaret.
   Allah's eyebrows cocked in assertion, waiting for 4:30.
   No smells inside but the sweaty feet and backs of black-
                                    robed tourists
   dignifying expected respect behind crafty cocked lenses,
                                    shutter-fed.

A gat-toothed guide.
  Whimsically directed, you're taken to pale-white rafters.
  Pulpit and corduroy lined mats are Northward arranged.
  A fence-lined section, small and matless, disappoints.
  "For the women: small", the Guide smiles.

After-thought and segregate.
  You slip your Hawian flip-flops on.
  And into Little India. Suri harem competing heads adjusting
  floral necklaces. Each grinning face behind
  a mayor of the moment. East promises; West receives.

Pulsing Punjabi; Bollywood blaring.
  Under, over, in and out. Inscrutable rainbow lined shops.
  Under crumbling Colonial balcony, a whirl of tea and saris.
  The *satu ringit* water souvenirs along with
  broken Bahasa Malayu; a *Salamat Tinggal* to a laugh.

And jutting jetties of the George Town harbour.
  Colonise with cultural effluence the shit-stabilised fishing boats.
  Under hastily harried stilts, plastic bucket buttress flat.
  Old women weaving under umbrellas, up, down, around.
  Rusting bicycles squat with huts harassing each other.

Beams buckle.
  Rain and foot struts. *Cold drinks* and trinkets
  from a thirteen year old supervised by a tea-supping grandma.
  Strut out, out into the sea. Penang's proud peopling.
  Hazy in the dog-lazy heat; the paradox of still bustle.

Squatting.
  With the beige-clad old man
  who gazes out to sea under an arthritic sun-salute.
  Whose picture you took away with you
  to keep and tell.

Pathology of Laterality

i.m. clarity of thought

The means for thought assemble now
askance, oblique, through dimmed eyes.
Flanking by cursory sidelines
and filtered through forethought,
you come.
Like so many decisions,
you awkwardly awaken,
a half-life kindled in unorthodoxy,
or *at-leasts* and the urge to such.
Whose heir apparent here fuels and mimics
these means? You are, as ever,
a caricature of decisiveness.

While you are attained through familiar
passages to thought, you're only warmed up
clarity, a mincing sidedish *claritas*,
sideways consumed.
You're only obligingly digested
and unfolded as solution.
Deciphered *here*, like a colonic exam,
are pitiful half-truths;
puckered fruits are unfulfilling.
Enough of a view, at least, to cause *a* pathos,
jarring enough to present in jars as such,
and, and firm enough to persuasively command
a cause and aetiology in so many words.
So, so very many words.

Wearied with hiding and peeking out from
eye-evading lines, you are vomited,
discrete though, and with a certain dignity.
The dignity of feigned certainty.
You are, alas, the bolus under palm shade
plopping with a plop on the plate
of conversation.
Stealthy, like a frog-in-the-throat,
you expectorant! Cleaving a clearing
before the alarm of speech.
A-hem. A-hem.
Materialise in a moment's politic
after having paced the labyrinth halls
of stutter and the grooves of a tongue-tip.
Pathetically emerge
naturally inaccurate,
inarticulate as description.
You, thought, are bowel-forged,
curved through, over and out
from the erstwhile depths;
settled on for seconds best.

    Look, out from Wardour street it strides;
    whilom glanced on the switch-way to pride.
    Ruminant, it's chewed and half-tried.
    Its pathological laterality we must abide.

People's Aptness in Experience
for PAE

You who are becoming
a way of being
seem to me apt.
You who are becoming
a way to be,
teach the apt
as if you who are
becoming a way
to be was always
and should be.

As I ponder
if my space utilisation
is purpose fit,
is apt to order,
I reflect that,
you who are to me
becoming a way
to be are apt;
if the purpose of
my space fits the
apt utilisation of
imaginings.

The data from
the space utilisation
survey reports
aptness at every

felt level. And I
experience it as
you becoming
a way of being
seeming appropriate
to my imaginings,
to hopes and expectations.

For, you are becoming
a way of being
with fit-for-purpose
space aptly utilised are
like that
love
whose space is so
apt to my rapt and
open-armed
space in which I
become and find
a way of finally,
finally being.

Poetry with an Hedge

For MB and the P&E posse, 8th May 2013

A spirit did my humble seal,
I'm glad for human peers.
For words which – half increate,
half received – forge a kind of *oikos*.

Leavened 'tween the bosom
Of thoughts and orts champed,
Here is a soupçon that is eco-
enough to outflank the right on.

Carefree in the crafted spree,
Edgy talk knocks the fluff off,
While enunciated complications
Prevent the ever-reticent a frame lock

With frame lock. An ecolodge of empathy
Opens with sallies fit for purposes.
Here is smallish and quite beautiful,
But not anthropomorphically cute.

Why choose the short form -
Squat in a thought box -
And not the emphatic sprawl
Of the projected nursed to state?

Something epistemological in a
Sandwich topple, a poets' lunch,
a launch of self to staunch the tea sigh with
tinkling teacups. An ethics of conveyance.

Conversation is navigable via the turn-take.
Politeness carves its compass points
Through gestural etiquette scratched
lightly in the gentle cartographies of

ink-spills, expressing what the words
in which we are living are *doing*.
Groping for a language with which to flex,
Through which to fetch, specificity.

The group grope is so much more
Friendly than the solitary fumble
Which is always prone to fleet satiation,
The ego prop on the rustic typecast.

An ecology of the disparate humbles *here*,
Troubling the slowly violent words of disciplinarity
Into visibility. Where the wood *and* trees
Are seen with the pleasurable oscillation of scale.

Before language degrades into recognition,
We must outflank the irreducible
With *ducere;* making visible a mimetic
Generosity with badges worn as *logos*.

Quaint Restraint

It's a serious business this,
holding off cliché with energy
and with every feint of analysis; it's,
like, unleashing the possible in a silent-box,
shuttered from the muttered utter.

The dextrous musing asunder saunters,
all set to heart break
at the dawn's break.
Every monstrous moment – this
moment – is abstruse with clarity.

The boy may proclaim,
"It tastes like chicken"
and not mean it implicitly,
or allusively; but it is both:
contractually zeitgeist.

Hierarchies of recognition entrench
to paralysis a simple "love" or,
the easier, "indifference".
A phatic burp betrays a social
dance-ease of convo over football's lingo.

Recognising ease is so, so hard,
as if happiness – or its effusive actions –
are ever-unearned; never learned.
Passive, the votives of repose
impose on those prim-roses.

Easy, the solitary poise
resists the uninflected toe-run;
a simple manoeuvre of defiantly
wearing sunglasses at dusk or
confidently trumpeting a nose-blow.

Present in absentia, you are
a circle to the social squared.
Harpy enough to circle-fulfil
with every breath-transaction;
coiled to name-exchange non surplus.

Trusting, implicitly, terror
trembles the psycho-legacy;
the mould of confirming phrases.
To onlook is to outlook, to
hook to inanity like harm.

Tuck in, tuck in, tuck in
dig in, dig in, dig in.
The maws and satiated grins
array the unselfconscious
it's so, so hard to affect.

Rise to Order
for B. P.

I

Rational, these isles tumble under rain and pleasant brisks
from abroad, clamming in via networks semi-conducive and
compelling. Extreme concern expands and worstens the hearths
of a country balancing smarter socialism with surveil-lances perked,
becoming an edgy parade of loaned lines and quick-ripened
truncheons.
Militants survey definitions rising out from the abstract,
prick-pocked map, pawn-shifting mortal threats whilst hit-
costs vitiate a legacy and decisions wince with recognition.
Opposition and opposing views provide fiscal family pains,
budget and fathom cyclic numbers as efficiency-
savings unravel in the rubbish piling on the street corners.

As ever, concrete comes to the rescue after which fossils claim
future word bodies, imprinted by aid handing out medicaments.
It always happens whilst pilgrims insouciantly stroll, wrists
tied away from their body like he's fishing for compliments.
It's a victory, as predicted, and no more de-spiriting for that,
where clouds of doubt cleanse and the hard-fought fireworks
& champagne sings overheads, showering a crowd's crowns
with grim assignation: keep me secure with statistics, O Lord.
Maws gape for places, placards, placebos with which the country
churns futures lining edu-queues, miserable and knowing it.

II

In form and in crease and, well edited, make as if to convince.
It spreads amid the panic of etymology which connects
such controversy and is ceremonial after all. Memorialise.
Franchise and transfer pulsating flags oddly.
Comrades in clean-washed foisted fears lament with a piper
                                                    tempering
the no-gos. This changes the banner-up expenses liberally
                                                    scattered
over the wire. "There are *very* big changes," forcing, squeezing
big, fat words through corset-training, pursued by a whipped
cream smile referring to faces mag-nameless and pixel-pocked.
It's not a headline, but South America boils off eggs with defective
chicken juice and with without-washed dirty brown hands.
Deservedly.

Today, sagely, the Ministry of Concern prepares a palliate dish of
capital numbers to bamboozle into bankruptcy a billion bears.
      *Like, we must look at **new** genetics.*
      Like, solar powered beef and sheep.
Such luminous partnerships collapse, owing support networks,
and benefit, clamouring onto pathways and shut down-turns.
Red still expelled after spies leak relations honourably
mini-skirted and with a servile grimace, traipsed a hard-won.
Central justice surprises with a car's aplomb
injuring a leg-acy blood-won aegis ago and stutter-
assaulted on eyes all over a world fashioned out of
Styrofoam, penicillin and those, like, small, circuit-board things.
Hiving was a sleight of hand last manufactured
in 1914, but generations have receded in shared shelves,

popping piano wires like sweets and exporting niches
backwards via auctions, beat and nick swap-meets and leisure
                                                    hours.

III

It spurts through a *journalese* of human shields,
trotting to the pale pace of intention. Peace beckons it
with brave military logic making it humanitarian. It
becomes the gurn of the opposition also taking to the
streets after a president looks to be tramping down where
broken glass can still be discerned. It rounds people up
despite the declared amnesty *alleging* brutality
with a megaphonic smile behind which a
a young journalist phrases a cower, lexi-dextrous.
She *is* under conditions so a lawyer proxies diligently
filling detail with such things as 'flash-mob' and 'ring-
leader' represented against *alleged* torture mimeod and
caveat in mind-swap palimpsest denial also
pricked and alert in spinnied concessions.

Such Easter doxology excludes unless
demands are met over *alleged* minority and wealth gaps.
Throw me economic impoverishment and I'll show you a
slice of my report-back. Fuck the watershed and ownership
and mark-up the training manual where points create profit.
This is the biggest *alleged* bank I could find, a prison
for banjaxed words. Forensic science can't help
but down-play the *alleged* enabler via institutional malaprop.
Hands up to positive discrimination, sold off in a compositional
regime change over which criticism jigs its prescribed dance.
Where who you know becomes a technical know-who.
Beneficent artworks, really facing buying chunks,
serving the family-owned, family-run platters as convincing
aperitif despite the *alleged* black pudding Sunday mourning wretch.

Thrive in new wake-up jingle and make possible
by positive thought, cronyism and surety of countenance.
Education skips the heart homewards in pathologies
shared indexically with a good night's sleep for all.
Sooth-settle under dark-art banners of controversy
which constitute the survival and sense-made of the here and now.
Power *alleges* in the bomb-bright dawn and startles in a child's face.

Sore

λυπάμαι

The word resonates as
a stone in the wayward rise
and river, lodging and latching,
addressing the elemental with *elan*
and causing – through conscience –
a calamity of rare vintage to mulder.

Words cannot cause the crippled affect
to articulate or iron out;
control is the watchword;
coming out-there is scary.
Risk risks in virtuous moral crunch.

The cycle of
aggression / chastisement / aggression / regret
which, of course, reproduces a cycle
too familiar in newsy by-lines,
preened for public defacement.

Contempt is a flexible term
applicable to self and to others,
filtered through self onto others.
Bile-like omissions wretch-up, wrangling
and jangling with cliché on the nerve-ends.

All this stuff produces a filtrate
of after-births and bi-products
of sanctimony and disharmony.
And the soreness and mutual shell-shock.
And anger is alienating.

Standards of Revolt

Apex is reached by pulling from gutter depth,
filtering the limpid fury beneath sentiment
and aching out solemnity like angel words.
These are the mantra warnings and cross-words,
threaded between and through which school dinners
feed morality. Tapping through on the mono-dial,
through eighties' off-sense and balancing, money
off-sets the surfeit with the *elan* and breeze brought
on pop-lyrics determinedly determine.
Beginners please ease out the banner hopes to
deride and decry an institution leaving sense alone.
– *"Leave 'im alone, Danny, ee's not wurf i'"* –
Motile, the sweaty palm conveys and betrays
a visual polygraphia, arched in marched words.
Pungent in the off-shot vomit, like feeling
crushed, knotted, raging inward and exclusive
in it at another mention of "the economy"
or its virgin agent, "the market".
I mean totally sick, not faux malodorous,
existential navel gazing or perma-anx
embodied by useless quip and Woody Allen.
I mean revising all the rhythmic routines as flourish,
as well as the tendentious reactions
ill-informed and half-formed.
Like every sentence you read is a
feather-swished elsewhere
and you no longer harbour the ruddy, rude-health
truths the flush of youth enabled.
Like, this is real life. Loathing it. Understand?

Somehow others' answers have always,
you know, accessed the painfully denied formula.
In a cheap haze, booze expensive
false culture or cultures, like, develop and deepen
on contact with the palate imploring fidelity.
Words before sense equal sentence.
Brandished, fed-back, limp and lacking
but it will have to do, have to do.
Such, like, real tragedy in these booths
in which the after–revolutionaries slouch and
couch louche thoughts to out hawk barter positions.
Revolting all over the table after too much whiskey.

The difficulty of cuddly toys
is their indomitable lack of clean,
their disgusting black-tipped,
frayed and fiddled-with fur
knowing not where it has been.
Which is like your words, David.
As if we need such semi-daily
reminders of what waste there is
up there or down there.
And especially your unwitting puns,
press-panned past in haste and hemistich.
Opinions, here, comfort
like the opposite faces feigning chaste.
You choose, you know,
which posture creates over-zealous postulates.
And the fuggy beer enables an emphatic determination
that the daylight cites as such and shrivels.
Problem is the tetra-pack phrases, like,
daily showed or revealed one step beside a quip.
Satire is nonsense: comfort accessed in faux negative.
Circumscribed, the standards of revolt are fed down

– trickling, perhaps –
becoming like the jumper ease which slightly pleases
but doesn't provide the dynamic ease of access of a cardigan.
Safe in their standards of revolt, adult-children bicker.

To Writ

Erotic imply
spry secret
impish in
ink writ
silent slit
to whit
through wit
in it
splay, array
deprave by
persuade betray
harden to cast
in jut jaw
fall out, plenty
and drip too, like,   like
         it's
                    perfect
through you
secrete self,
such self almost
too much true to
be wry, awry, try
mawkish through
on to channel wake
with bent nape
with bib for dribble
forth more bite
in incisive insight
a clinch of glue

for you who
wrench-come
on the sly.

Trending Bad Body Language

Traipsed in the roomy imaginings
of a moment in this metropolis,
each sly step affirms its bosom
proud and formed in eye gaze.
Material grips to bottom swagger.
At what expense the fine and febrile
towards this event of the preened self?
Imagine in the fantasy bloom of stuff
and observe the baroque effort.

The sum of some equals torture,
as if facial effort and glum
agonise to be natural.
Being self-styled like baby bliss;
uninflected or interred in the corpse-savvy
danger of make-up or down.
Fine and busy to be murmuring silent,
a-cursing others of trending.

Shop windows halo steps, caught
in the out-of-corner regal stance;
smoothly swing at unlimited tries
to become just this:
the strut with the bump proudly,
smugly elasticised under loosened shirt;
the murmur of mummy on form.
Whatever God and stripe is ephemera these days
she wants all of it, spun to the eternal like nylon.

Pigeon toes and faux feys
abound in this metropolis.
A trade in whimsy has the market
overwhelmed.
Along this feral street designed feet fleet,
self-imposed importance and skinny time;
lattéd in transient crêpe drape.

Fine words abandon and fixate elsewhere.
And the baby murmur?
An attractive opposition,
a contrast relief like German nouns.
Action and being is sapped by writing
gerunds when static, bum humbling.

Classes have muddled so much
in this metropolis –
with faux-p and received enunciation,
the access all areas, the natty clothes
and adverto-ironies –
that the driven, solitary aim seems
sentimental or part of a kitsch analogy,
like dial-up, Tetris or the cassette tape phone case.

Unsubtle and unsupple blunt sounds
terrorise the try and sap energy,
as if emotion hooks harass and tear
the seeming to make single sense
from the immense panorama
of utility and managese.

Sensate, the harridans are out
to have you with their
verb-slight and lexi-violence,
designed to chew through you,
to swell tongues,
to vandalise your eyes
and scandalise the tries at the natural.
They are our critical resistance gone mad.

So the fear-bustle and
squabble-struggle of it overwhelms.
Finding no solace in architecture
– this regal pissing pot –
or the dignified beauty of crumbled arches.
Touch not the tear-drop window frame
labour-lathed and delicate.
Because the bullshit cache is full-brimmed
and his body language and phrases interpose:

> *"You wouldn't use bad language*
> *with customers;*
> *so don't use bad body language."*

Two poems involving love

30th June, 2013

I

Processing the arch voice intrusions,
Care wafts like the fly curve-flight
Away and into the balmy calm.
Its robust authenticity becomes a metaphor
For a felt moment described as content
But distrusted as such.
Your smooth and shrub-scraped thighs distract
To refrain the perfection of the afternoon
And the moments comprising present.
Surprisingly unrecognisable languages sound frame
Unwittingly the semblance of coming into each other;
They are crucial as a way of making expression.
That dress that I equivocally prompted you into
Frames a body I'm acquainting every thought with.
A casual hand, flecked red as lips,
Centres an explanation of the content,
A temper to the restless,
A reminder that waits end.

GF

II

Plants do do that – I know – as I've seen it. I know that plants do
do that and still I need you to confirm that plants do do that. Your
touch, your nose, a fragment of tissue, I've seen a man resembling
the man I wanted when I didn't know. And now I know that plants
do do that, that that is not this man, that I want to confirm that
plants do do that, as I've seen it, that you are not that man, not that
that man that says that plants do do that, but mine.

EK

Motion Study: **A Method for Increasing the Efficiency of the Workman. Or, Applied Etymology for the Workplace.**

Sussex Univesity, 8th March, 2008
After the Gilbreths, 1922

A

Its aim is the finding and perpetuation of the schemes of perfection.
Practice makes. Shine shoes, clean teeth, scrub behind your.
The three potentially agitating and violent stages in this process will be:

1. Discovering and classifying best practice
2. Deducing the laws
3. Applying the laws to standardised practice.

Time-tried methods and indubitable logic to make a dynastic bed-rock.
So all manner of walking imprints the counterfoil and will be kept under
wraps for future scrutiny. It will be possible to depict dynamically the
position of the femoral head at any time. The reflexive has its own
definite place in the evolution of scientific management. It's our vision
that such collateral is transformed from needless, ill-directed and
ineffective motion into something else entirely.
Heads down lads, and wait for my signal.

It's a method of attacking the possible, the potential, the
otherwise utterly wasted and re-packaging it for the local
movement. Call them contractions (especially of fluid, but
generally of man). Contain, restrict, rescind, redistribute.

NEWTONIAN INTERJECTION 1:

Body   contin   ues in   a state   of rest
less it   is act   ed on   exter   nal force

Toilet stop – your bodily functions are bad credit –
but they are usually found to have been voided
from the splenic flexure onwards. It's going to require
good, hard study, but the vision is for an
Ultimate system. That's a capital U with tremendous savings
for a limited time. Everything's been considered.
These are the exhaustive variables of the workmen:

1. Anatomy
2. Brawn
3. Contentment
4. Creed
5. Earning power
6. Experience
7. Fatigue
8. Habit(s)
9. Health
10. Mode of Living (see Health)
11. Nutrition (see Health and Mode of Living and Habits)
12. Size (see Anatomy and Brawn)
13. Skill (see Earning power)
14. Temperament (see Creed)
15. Training.

How neat to alphabeticalise assets in such a tidy way to.
How to control these variables? Perhaps you could start
with the lunch box, ensuring the working man has enough
    (*shhhh, it's brown bread not white*).
Splice life to evince proportionate sums. Equations

whose lateral co-workers rework themselves as inevitable, or natural, neutral. Schematise and study 'til scrutiny enables a 'neaten up' of extraneous factors. *Neutralise that eye mote with* EYE BLITZ™ *Refreshing, energising liquid to blink away your* co-efficients. We must essay an immediate streamlining of bodies badly bungled.

Phalanxes of hunch-backed men discuss their very own biceps and compare them against the stats in *Worker's Weekly*. They know, of course, (we are just working for their benefit) that there are also variables of Surroundings and Equipment and Tools and Motion. All of which, to counteract any irregular movement, must be mixed with sweat, worked up into a caricature of a good Bolshevik and *Krasnaya-Gazeta* mâchéd all over, including the other variables:

Acceleration – Automaticity – Combinatory – Cost
– Direction – Effectiveness – Footpounds of work
accomplished – Overcoming inertia – Length – Necessity
– Path – Play for Position – Speed

This gifts a whole other tool-box of control.
The free terms under which we labour, through which we trudge.
Or, they may free the terms in which we turn. Or, freedom
means optimizing each term. When you begin to examine it from say.
At each successive point the occupation of a different position,
enabled by this study, is thoroughly democratic actually.
We begin to see as with panoptic lenses – spider eyes espy lies –
knowing, being always of it, what position is played for.

But most of our illustrations are drawn from brick-laying, so our conclusions based on this data-set could be too local, making application obsolete nowadays, do you agree? Well, do you agree? Unless – but perhaps there is – a 'transcendent' worker or something perennial evoked here. Extract from the promise of conjecture a cow and an acre for all. Take those who don't fit into the village hall as silent on this issue. And so on into someone's merry dance of militant production. This has passed through all eras of history, practiced by nations barbarous and civilised, and ended up with this proposition:

the Councell shalbe assented vnto.

So just lay your [   ] bricks and let me do the.
Was the implication, or imprecation.

We'll show you a way in which these diagrams can help.
Tip your hat.
No?
We'll show you *the* way in which *those* diagrams *will* help.
Tip your hat.
No?!
The modern day flat cap is the tap on the rear
with the burrowing jingle as accompaniment.

B

NEWTONIAN INTERJECTION 2

*The rate of change of mo mentum purports
direct ion as the force acting on it*

Imbibe so (one man's 'natural' is another man's) it becomes "on
impulse".
Though the fingers feeling for the pulse check the code.
Read against the manual whose fissure-faced grinning pictograms
assure: the faster the motion, the more output. But the challenge
remains that very few can read a map effectively without
orienting it in the direction. So we're told – vague attempts at flexing,
contorting yourself, refined in such a way as so to indoctrinate a
radicality of limbs; one in front the other 'round the exercise yard.
My maniples can be identified by their reliably straight backs.
Sworne to their seruice, and wedded to their willes.
Not looking awry or skewing word unless it pleases;
a little tap here and the horse obeys the cart.

Stuff your union rules for a moment. They were always plebiscite and
hindrance to standardisation, frankly. And, here, have a handful of
artificially restricted maximum outputs for your time. One man's battle
fatigue is another. It all depends what X stands for. The question
What will **you** *do with* **your** *time?* scrolls past on pitch-side barriers.
Which is the start of a process whose internal logic runs:

How will you spend your time?
How much will you spend on your time?
How much you expend on our time is not your decision to make.

Contained in your social activities are the kernels of. Which leads, in their version, to an account of roped limbs in Virginia.

> *3 Feb 2007: On Friday The House of Delegates*
> *unanimously approved a resolution expressing*
> *"profound regret" for Virginia's role in the slave*
> *trade.*

The white man's burthen being, here, expending valuable energy on another waste-of-time lynching.

C

ROLL UP, ROLL UP, for
Pompes, Pageants, Motions & Masques

Queue up, plug in. The script-cues for this night's puppet show are
brought to you by
  [UNKNOWN]
Colours, such colours, this light-show will enrapture, dumbfound.
"I found him like this, I did, I swear".
Such excellent and indirect effects of entertainment.
For example, we've even given them a ping-pong table as a
compensation for will (though they didn't even know they had
one, ergo, how lucky they are). There's virtue in macro-mimicry.
Whereas *vnto men's inward cognitions, vnto priuie intents of their
harts, religion serueth for a bridle* (I always say).
Believe such advocacy – *your rights, our fight* – move
                    towards, in, through it.
You'll know what to do when the clock-off moment comes.
Receiving this always-already routine
(*a-one,two,three; one,two,three; one,two,three,one*)
with an insouciance bordering on pathology.
Saying: I freely take this lawfully wedded
of my own accord and really, really meaning it.
Believe in the truth-content of these stagey distractions.
They've cost a lot and we didn't *have* to.

D

NEWTONIAN INTERJECTION 3
Re act   when one   exerts   a force   equal
an opp   osite   on an   other   body

Kenesis produces, not least upon frenzied examination of its Greek roots.
All such postulations amount to the question: how much, and how many, was it? "Round it down", says a tubercular voice from the Sovereign's corner.

> *The bombs killed as many as 140,000*
> *people in Hiroshima and 80,000 in*
> *Nagasaki by the end of 1945. Since then,*
> *thousands more have died from injuries*
> *or illness attributed to exposure to*
> *radiation released by the bombs. In both*
> *cities, the overwhelming majority of the*
> *dead were civilians.*

See where this has gotten us, says the ersatz liberal voice. Who knows what 'this' is, in her illustration? So that's a conservative 250,000 in locomotion from one state to quite another's dream. Imperceptible in its insidious spread in the minutiae of verbal exchanges, until this is no longer a 'contract' but much more of a. Such studied invention! Making possible the shift from acting for to acted upon without the slightest notice. You'll be immortalised in the flourish of kinematic graphics and charts wherein crucial fluctuations are, at first, "exploited", but later reasoned as "contained".

Strap yer kinetic boots on and act busy
(especially if you've got nothing to do).
Understand it as a stave, a grid, a notation
borne of an idea in the mind of the Prime
Mover. All aboard and all towards the upward
helix of progress which is a common
elision prompting instruction carved
as keep-sakes on tablets which promise
to be as addictive as those catchy maxims:

The inside plank of a bricklayer's platform must extend.
A first-class labourer can do his work with a straight back.
Contentment affects the output of a worker.
Or, a favourite: *"You can't teach an old dog new tricks" may be*
heard around the world. While this may be true with dogs, it is not
true with workmen.

Distilled to a pap-like state so as to be supped along with the
illusion of our 5 a day.

Part of a balanced.

Insisting on motive as a way of vaguely "being there".
The moment's productivity becomes:
        my time – my pay – my dues.
Autonomously extract the granite from the pavements of your own
neighbourhood to line the North's. The explanation is there in the
fine. If only you'd chose to read it. Fear-driven, the Cold stare,
the imagination's picture of insurrection gives Masser the heebie-
jeebies. Like, have you read *Slave Life in Georgia: A Narrative of the*
Life, Sufferings, and Escape of John Brown, a Fugitive Slave?
I have, well, I skimmed it, and knowledge is forewarned power.

The possibility of heads up from digging and that damned singing is enough motive. This is to be your first language, your necessitated mother tongue.

Silence.

E

To conclude, I hope you'll allow that this has all been for the best. In the meantime, while we are waiting for the politicians and educators to realise the importance of this subject and to create the bureaus and societies to undertake and complete the work, we need not be idle. We have a scientific method of attack and I assure you, sir, the results will be of an exacting standard.

Yours faithfully,

POSER PINE'S ARTIFICIAL GARDEN

CAUTION

SLIPPERY WHEN WET

i.m. VF-T

i.

I was peddling my trusty deception down Blatchington road,
keeping an ear open for the threatening mumblings of desire.
The breeze unsettled my equilibrium as I straddled the lamppost,
chaining memory and desire to the chiselled dusk.
The rain shattered startles into the humming street.
 "I told you moments ago," muttered a teenaged mum
on the down low, a helmet of hair atop her head,
a 21st century Dolores through whom humanity poureth.
I found myself thrumming the inalienable to Khadeeth's Mart
perked in self-persuasion of 'conscience',
turning to the dark demesne of the entrance which failed to.

ii.

Inside, the false prophet promises of cowardly collage made the walls,
stating something codified, for the recondite alone.
Britney waved the airways, oddly,
replacing the synthetic with the authority of authenticity;
my crumpled heart bore time with Britney.
A speech of welcome imposed itself on me from great, tight corners,
from an incongruously placed seraph sampling happiness quotes.
In the twilight of a damp day and the dark time of a shop fray,
vainly my eyes on signs they rested where:
"Enterprise rent-a-goat" promised good time and conscience rebate;
and *"I had a love affair with a statue"* feigned off-the-wall wit.
Strange this list before me which marked 'needs must'
to which I, in turn, did state my trajectory.
I followed this as if compelled to fill out supple sighs.
These bags that last I saw in Tesco rumpled
pleasingly against my thigh with no mere smugness.
Feeling myself ennobled, I sallied forth.

iii.

Trudging to the veg. display, arrayed and arraigned in tragi-delight,
I had pick of things leafy and gorged on the fullness, it seemed, of death.
Fruits, round and perfumed like breasts and tender to the touch.
My melancholy eyes divine did catch a glimpse of
her amidst the grown-green garden vegetables,
this familiar compound ghost I seemed always to pass:
the triple-flavoured goddess Koré.
Through her I felt I had emerged
and the world was now grey-green
with my breath.
Looking at the foul awe of her,
I mumbled that she hadn't met me yet.

"You who exhaust all epithets," I declaimed,
"achingly vivid, still pirouette before me like you used to,
flouncing over, Oh, the severed head of John
he who will baptise no more on this earth."

iv.

In the next aisle, an ancient man, always reactionary and never
content with the white printer paper in aggressive stacks
before him; the printer ink a generational insult.
The absent aisle, I remarked, is like an absent life through
which all threatens; thuggish moments apt to give out orders.
I furtively checked my face in a mirror with stars on it
next to towels folded like ptyx and soaps smug with clean.
Aesthetic practitioners in every aisle, needy wielding.
Women looking stuffed into themselves
like they've forgotten how to be.
A man with thermometer earrings and a fine profile
echoed past me and I was reminded of
the omnipresence of wit and the nostalgia
of wielding the f-bomb like a status symbol.
Whom should persuasion summon here
to sooth the shrug of my passion? I wondered.
In the corner a furtive teenager twitched,
gripping a pocket pack of handy randys
and with a tellingly tapering grin.
Women in brood competition abounded.
A T-shirt bearing the deathly slogan,
You don't have to be posh to ski here but it helps
sauntered before a ready-real trolley.
Pressures of style came from every angle,
especially melancholy mine,
leaving a middle vacuum where voice used to be,
leaving a vacuum to hoover up time.
Fourteen varieties of Britain's favourite tea, I thought,
I being ever sick in the safety of anguish!
That moment I realised that I was sick of biology,
and of the awkwardness which burns deep and chaifs.

Stopping off in an aisle of pre-packaged feelings,
I feigned to rest a little from praise and grievous pleasure and pain.
Willingly, I sampled pain on a cocktail stick
proffered by that hoary cripple with a malicious eye
who seemed to follow me with it. And with words:
"Just as much you wonder if I mean just what I say,
that's just how much I question the social games you play.
Just as much as you wonder 'bout me staring back at you,
that's just how much I question the silly things you do."

In the next aisle I grabbed a Tetra pack of lifestyle to stabilise.
Then in my bare palm was found a jar of olives.
Holding the jar up to the light, its contents became
indistinguishable from the epiphanies unreached
on the imagined dust of the top shelf.

V.

About the frozen foods I fleet footed,
and moved to pick up an icy word filter promising
"un sens plus pur aux mots de la tribu".
Like the last time, I didn't believe a word of it.
By chance, a swan's beak and black foot were captive
in the ice compartment next to the lollies.
White was the ice I saw in this icicle–icy ice drawer.
My hand reached down,
my fingernails scraped the ice
like Onyx.

vi.

There at the fish counter,
where all mackerel seemed dead
pricy enough to incite a riot, I pondered.
I doubted myself of my doubtful dreams.
That, the 'monger reminded me,
was Mister Nomer
casting a sturgeon into the pot as he spoke.
Fishes mouths lay 'ope,
looking like they couldn't cope with life.
I picked up a packet of Marine Breeze cod fillets.
Oh to be an angel fish!

vii.

Approaching the self-mirroring monstrous eyelid of the deli counter,
I caught a projective self in the aspiration of the ticket dispenser
and thought of the finest logos I could cope with.
"Ah, cold meats," I intoned,
"you beasts, having died, thou art as Hesperus,
giving new splendour to the dead,
and make for a fine picnic spread."
Now more than ever seems it rich to fry,
especially when back-bacon's on discount.

viii.

And then to wine, where the I of the confidently suave
developed strategies to confront the social world,
through allegory and various shades of willy pose.
Attempting to extract fine sentiment from its carapace
of parataxis, I ascended to the shiny heights of self-identity,
kicking pricks and chicks into the dust of vein society.
There was no turning back and the end was in sight.
A bottle of slick wine selected for the later Toast funèbre.

ix.

Disappointingly, I failed to elicit a dry smile from
a sullen steward of fruit and servility,
the cruellest combination;
'twas a pale Galilean at the till.
I was doing something to change by calling for it.
I faced up to a kindly reality that seemed always eager to please.
I spoke transaction with a voice from the tomb itself.

X.

Gathering my goods, I tripped to the exit
where the revolution of the door was devouring children.
My knees bent, I desperately stooped to carry.
Walking out into the balmy-now dusk,
I wondered why
even the most beautiful,
even precisely the beautiful,
has today become a lie.
I tipped the ash of my cigar into the art-tray
to gather there like iron filings;
roses again to bloom.
It was like Tournon nights outside
and each step into the dusk was like a shower.
One stiff blind horse awaited me dutifully, his blessed bones a-stare.
And Mary, my beauty, lingered nearby, imagining my heroic return.
All at once, our feet and hooves expressed joy
and we turned to finally gave nothingness the slip,
once more to hurry home.